2/15

RAINBOW IN THE CLOUD

Center Point
Large Print

**This Large Print Book carries the
Seal of Approval of N.A.V.H.**

RAINBOW IN THE CLOUD

The Wisdom and Spirit of
MAYA ANGELOU

CENTER POINT LARGE PRINT
THORNDIKE, MAINE

This Center Point Large Print edition
is published in the year 2015 by arrangement with
Random House, an imprint and division of
Random House LLC.

Text sources can be found on page 135. Photograph
permissions can be found on page 141.

The text of this Large Print edition is unabridged.
In other aspects, this book may vary
from the original edition.
Printed in the United States of America
on permanent paper.
Set in 16-point Times New Roman type.

ISBN: 978-1-62899-453-7

Library of Congress Cataloging-in-Publication Data

Angelou, Maya.
[Works. Selections]
Rainbow in the cloud : the wisdom and spirit of Maya Angelou / Maya
Angelou. — Center Point Large Print edition.
pages ; cm
Summary: "More than 200 of Dr. Angelou's most pivotal quotes
organized in themed sections—from sage advice and beautiful stanzas to
humorous quips and pointed observations—drawn from each of her
published works and from her social media posts. Also featured are
special words of wisdom she shared with her family, handpicked by her
son, Guy Johnson"—Provided by publisher.
ISBN 978-1-62899-453-7 (library binding : alk. paper)
1. Angelou, Maya—Quotations. 2. Quotations, American.
   3. Large type books. I. Title.
PS3551.N464A6 2015
818'.5409—dc23
                                                          2014041778

For
Lydia Stuckey

"When it looked like the sun
wouldn't shine anymore
God put a rainbow in the clouds."

—CHRISTIAN SPIRITUAL

CONTENTS

RAINBOW IN THE CLOUD

CHILDHOOD
&
PARENTHOOD

A child's talent to endure stems from her ignorance of alternatives.

Everything of value takes work, particularly relationships. If a mother and daughter don't understand each other, and further don't have sympathy for each other's lack of understanding then the task is to build a bridge across the chasm of misunderstanding.

Home is the nest where children are raised and the place where they are the most important inhabitants. In homes in which this is not true, the parents are not making the sacrifices which are necessary.

I believe that one can never leave home. I believe that one carries the shadows, the dreams, the fears and dragons of home under one's skin, at the extreme corners of one's eyes, and possibly in the gristle of the earlobe.

I love my son and I loved him when he was growing up, but I was not in love with him which means that I did not dote and I was willing to make the hard decisions. One should never let the love of one's child prevent or hinder the vital and necessary work of parenting.

If our children are to approve of themselves, they must see that we approve of ourselves.

Independence is a heady draft, and if you drink it in your youth it can have the same effect on the brain as young wine.

It is time for parents to teach young people early on that in diversity there is beauty and there is strength. We all should know that diversity makes for a rich tapestry, and we must understand that all the threads of the tapestry are equal in value no matter their color; equal in importance no matter their texture.

Of all the needs (there are none imaginary) a lonely child has, the one that must be satisfied, if there is going to be hope and a hope of wholeness, is the unshaking need for an unshakable God.

Parents who tell their offspring that sex is an act performed only for procreation do everyone a serious disservice.

The ache for home lives in all of us, the safe place where we can go as we are and not be questioned.

The Black child must learn early to allow laughter to fill his mouth or the million small cruelties he encounters will congeal and clog his throat.

The command to grow up at once was more bearable than the faceless horror of wavering purpose, which was youth.

This is no longer my house, it is my home. And because it is my home, I have not only found myself healed of the pain of a broken love affair, but discovered that when something I have written does not turn out as I had hoped, I am not hurt so badly. I find that my physical ailments, which are a part of growing older, do not depress me so deeply. I find that I am quicker to laugh and much quicker to forgive.

Our young must be taught that racial peculiarities do exist, but that beneath the skin, beyond the differing features, and into the true heart of being, fundamentally, we are more alike, my friend, than we are unalike.

What child can resist a mother who laughs freely and often?

When I was young I often wondered how I appeared to people around me, but I never thought to see myself in relation to the entire world.

BLACK
IDENTITY

Although as Black people we had a dignity and a love of life, those qualities had to be defended constantly.

Although there was always generosity in the Negro neighborhood, it was indulged on pain of sacrifice. Whatever was given by Black people to other Blacks was most probably needed as desperately by the donor as by the receiver. A fact which made the giving or receiving a rich exchange.

Black Americans of my generation didn't look kindly on public mournings except during or immediately after funerals. We were expected by others and by ourselves to lighten the burden by smiling, to deflect possible new assaults by laughter. Hadn't it worked for us for centuries? Hadn't it?

Black entertainers have had to be ten times better than anyone else, historically.

Black women whose ancestors were brought to the United States beginning in 1619 have lived through conditions of cruelties so horrible, so bizarre, the women had to reinvent themselves. They had to find safety and sanctity inside themselves or they would not have been able to tolerate such torture. They had to learn quickly to be self-forgiving, for often their exterior actions were at odds with their interior beliefs.

Despite the harshness of their lives, I have always found that older Black women are paragons of generosity. The right plea, arranged the right way, the apt implication, persuade the hungriest Black woman into sharing her last biscuit.

How could I explain a young Black boy to a grown man who had been born White?

I do not believe the N word should be used at all . . . It is time to retire the N word and rely on our vocabulary to speak to people without calling them any racial pejorative at all.

I don't go for that hate talk. Negroes ain't got time to be hating anybody. We got to get together.

I was born to work up to my grave
But I was not born
To be a slave.

I, with millions of other Americans, have the same dream Martin Luther King Jr. had; when I wake up I wish some of the things I dreamt would be true. I wish that little Black and White boys and girls would hold hands without being shocked at their nearness to each other and say in a natural way, "We have overcome."

It was a traditional ruse that was used to shield the Black vulnerability; we laughed to keep from crying.

Malcolm X was America's Molotov cocktail, thrown upon the White hope that all Black Americans would follow the nonviolent tenets of Dr. Martin Luther King Jr.

Prejudice is a burden which confuses the past, threatens the future, and renders the present inaccessible.

Most Black Americans ridicule and revile the Uncle Toms they see on film and television or read about. What they don't realize is that these people stepped and fetched in a nation and time that it was hard for Black people to survive, much less find a decent job. Rarely is consideration given to the sacrifices these people made in order to feed their families, what it cost them in self-respect to make sure the next generation survived. It is these circumstances that make Mr. Paul Dunbar's poem, "We Wear the Mask," so poignant.

My people had used music to soothe slavery's torment or to propitiate God, or to describe the sweetness of love and the distress of loveless-ness, but I knew no race could sing and dance its way to freedom.

Since we were descendants of African slaves torn from the land, we reasoned we wouldn't have to earn the right to return, yet we wouldn't be so arrogant as to take anything for granted.

The drums began. The audience pounded out the rhythm, moving it, controlling and possessing the music, the orchestra, and me.

"Uh, uh, oh huh.
O yea, freedom,
Uh huh. Uh huh."

As the song ended, the small crowd thundered a hot appreciation. Even as I bowed, I knew the applause was only in a small part for me. I had been merely the ignition which set off their fire. It was our history, our painful passage and uneven present, that burned luminously in the dark theater.

The Africans say that "Only a fool points to his history with his left hand." What this means is that you must know and respect where you came from. How can you truly respect yourself if you do not know or understand the struggles and trials your people surmounted for you to be here?

The man who is a bigot
is the worst thing God has got.

Through the centuries of despair and dislocation, we had been creative, because we faced down death by daring to hope.

Unbidden would come the painful reminder— "Not all slaves were stolen, nor were all slave dealers European."

Unfortunately, fortitude was not like the color of my skin, given to me once and mine forever. It needed to be resurrected each morning and exercised painstakingly. It also had to be fed with at least a few triumphs.

We are not our brother's keeper; we are our brother and we are our sister. We must look past complexion and see community.

We must ask questions and find answers that will help us to avoid dissolving into the merciless maw of history.

Whites had been wrong all along. Black and brown skin did not herald debasement and a divinely created inferiority. We were capable of controlling our cities, our selves, and our lives with elegance and success. Whites were not needed to explain the working of the world, nor the mysteries of the mind.

AMERICA

African and Southern Black American women can exude a charm which acts as a narcotic on their targets.

Appearances to the contrary, there is a code of social behavior among Southern Blacks (and almost all of us fall into that category, willingly or not) which is as severe and distinct as a seventeenth-century minuet or an African initiation ritual. There is a moment to speak, a tone of voice to be used, words to be carefully chosen, a time to drop one's eyes, and a split-second when a stranger can be touched on the shoulder or arm or even knee without conveying anything more than respectful friendliness. A lone woman in a new situation knows it is correct to smile slightly at the other women, never grin (a grin is proper only between friends or people making friendship), and nod to unknown men. This behavior tells the company that the new woman is ready to be friendly but is not thirsting after another woman's mate. She should be sensual, caring for her appearance, but taking special care to minimize her sexuality.

Every family in our country has someone, a daughter, a son, a nephew, a niece, a cousin, who has served or is serving in the armed services.

These relatives have risked or are risking their lives in foreign places few of us have ever seen or can even spell. These heroes and sheroes deserve our heartfelt gratitude for holding the flag of freedom high in the foreign air.

If growing up is painful for the Southern Black girl, being aware of her displacement is the rust on the razor that threatens the throat.

I'm grateful to be an American. I am grateful that we can be angry at the terrorist assault on 9/11 and at the same time be intelligent enough not to hold a grudge against every Arab and every Muslim.

Our country is grieving. Each child who has been slaughtered belongs to each of us and each slain adult is a member of our family. It is impossible to explain the horror to ourselves and to our survivors. We need to hold each other's hands and look into each other's eyes and say, "I am sorry." —In response to the tragedy in Newtown, Connecticut, on December 14, 2012

I believe that there lives
a burning desire in the
most sequestered private
heart of every American,
a desire to belong to a
great country.

The South of the United States can be so impellingly beautiful that sophisticated creature comforts diminish in importance.

The Stars and Stripes was our flag and our only flag, and that knowledge was almost too painful to bear.

Values among Southern rural Blacks are not quite the same as those existing elsewhere. Age has more worth than wealth, and religious piety more value than beauty.

We must wage a ceaseless battle against the forces of greed and hatred which are the foundations of all political inequality.

*When cane straps flog the body
dark and lean, you feel the blow.*

COMMUNITY
&
CULTURE

All people use food for more reasons than mere nutrition.

Blithering ignorance can be found wherever you choose to live.

Don't be a prisoner of ignorance. The world is larger, far more complicated, and far more wonderful than ignorance allows.

Each one of us has lived through some devastation, some loneliness, some weather superstorm or spiritual superstorm; when we look at each other we must say, I understand. I understand how you feel because I have been there myself.

Hold those things that tell your history and protect them.

In an unfamiliar culture, it is wise to offer no innovations, no suggestions, or lessons. The epitome of sophistication is utter simplicity.

Often we feel we must have infuriated nature and it has responded by bringing havoc upon our communities. I think it is unwise to personalize nature. I think when we don't know what to do it's wise to do nothing. Sit down quietly; quiet our hearts and minds and breathe deeply.

Perhaps travel cannot prevent bigotry, but by demonstrating that all peoples cry, laugh, eat, worry, and die, it can introduce the idea that if we try to understand each other, we may even become friends.

> *Though there's one thing that I cry for*
> *I believe enough to die for*
> *That is every man's responsibility to man.*

Thus we lived through a major war. The question in the ghettos was, Can we make it through a minor peace?

The onus is upon us all to work to improve the human condition. Perform good deeds, for that is truly the way to battle the forces of entropy that are at work in our world. The composite of all our efforts can have an effect. Good done anywhere is good done everywhere.

Together, we may be able to plan a less painful future. Separate, we can only anticipate further ruptures and deeper loneliness.

We are social animals. When we unite in purpose, we are greater than the sum of our parts. Everything that divides or isolates us prevents and obstructs us from realizing our potential as a species.

LOVE
&
RELATIONSHIPS

A conversation between friends can sound as melodic as a scripted song.

Always be concerned when a naked man offers you his shirt; a person can't love you if he or she can't love him- or herself.

Boys seem to think that girls hold the keys to all happiness, because the female is supposed to have the right of consent and/or dissent. It's interesting that they didn't realize in those yearning days past, nor even in the present days of understanding, that if the female had the right to decide, she suffered from her inability to instigate. That is, she could only say yes or no if she was asked.

From the moment you leave this house, don't let anybody raise you. Every time you get into a relationship you will have to make concessions, compromises, and there's nothing wrong with that.

I am grateful that love exists: familial love (love between relatives), romantic love (a passion between lovers), agape love (divine love between God and friends), love of nature (the majesty of mountains, the lasting love of oceans), and the joy of laughter. We are stronger, kinder, and more generous because we live in an atmosphere where love exists.

I am truly grateful: for being here, for being able to think, for being able to see, for being able to taste, for appreciating love—for knowing that it exists in a world so rife with vulgarity, with brutality and violence . . . And I'm grateful to know it exists in me, and I'm able to share it with so many people.

I commend lovers, I am en-heartened by lovers, I am encouraged by their courage and inspired by their passion.

I try to plant peace if I do not want discord; to plant loyalty and honesty if I want to avoid betrayal and lies.

If we had the opportunity to talk about it, laboriously and painfully, I might have been forever lost in the romance of romance lost. But with no sounding board except my own ears and honest thoughts, I had to stop weeping.

Jealousy in romance is like salt in food. A little can enhance the savor, but too much can spoil the pleasure and, under certain circumstances, can be life-threatening.

Leers and lascivious smirks to the contrary, sensuality does not necessarily lead to sex, nor is it meant to be a substitute for sex. Sensuality is its own reward.

> *Love, by nature, exacts a pain*
> *Unequalled on the rack.*

Love liberates. It doesn't just hold—that's ego— love liberates!

Nothing will work unless you do.

I've learned that people will forget what you said, people will forget what you did, but people will never forget how you made them feel.

One can never know too many good people. One must be open to what life has to bring. I have learned that a friend may be waiting behind a stranger's smile.

The most called-upon prerequisite of a friend is an accessible ear.

The thorn from the bush one has planted, nourished, and pruned pricks most deeply and draws more blood.

There is an intimate laughter to be found only among friends.

When people speak with brutal honesty, what is most remembered is the brutality, not the honesty.

ART
&
LITERATURE

All great artists draw from the same resource: the human heart.

Art was the flower of life and despite the years of ill-treatment Black artists were among its most glorious blossoms.

Cooking is like writing poetry: Be careful in the choice of your ingredients and respectful of how they work together. That's true of all efforts in life.

Every experience shapes your writing, being stuck in a car on a lonely bridge, or dancing at a prom, being the it girl on the beach, all of those things influence your life, they influence how you write, and the topics you choose to write about.

For a person who grew up in the '30s and '40s in the segregated South, with so many doors closed to me without explanation, libraries and books said, "Here I am, read me." Take time to read.

I knew that words, despite the old saying, never fail. And my reading had given me words to spare.

I realized I was not a writer who teaches, but a teacher who writes.

I've had people explain to me what one of my poems meant, and I've been surprised that it meant that to them. If a person can use a poem of mine to interpret her life or his life, good. I can't control that. Nor would I want to.

If a little learning is dangerous, a little fame can be devastating.

In that little town in Arkansas, whenever my grandmother saw me reading poetry she would say, "Sister, Mama loves to see you read the poetry because that will put starch in your backbone."

Let me tell so much truth. I want to tell the truth in my work. The truth will lead me to the light.

Never put your sheroes and heroes up on pedestals; placing them on pedestals is setting yourself up for disappointment. You must take the good that people do and put the bright light on that good, but human beings can never withstand such light without showing their shadows and warts. All mortals have their shortcomings and weaknesses. Their skills and deeds are what we must applaud. Don't fall victim to the cult of personality.

Only poets care about what happened to the snows of yesteryear.

Some entertainers have tried to make art of their coarseness, but in their public crudeness they have merely revealed their own vast senses of personal inferiority. When they heap mud upon themselves and allow their tongues to wag with vulgarity, they expose their belief that they are not worth loving and in fact are unlovable.

There was going to be a storm and it was a perfect night for rereading *Jane Eyre*.

We must be suspicious of censors who say they mean to prohibit our art for our own welfare.

Without the presence and energy of art in our lives, we are capable of engaging in heartless activities without remorse and cruelties with clear consciences.

There is no greater agony than bearing an untold story inside you.

SPIRITUALITY

Faith and prayer are important elements of my belief in God. Faith is my rock, but it is also the way I align my thoughts, my heart, and my actions to realize my goals. Prayer is the way I connect with the energy of God, it is also the way I clarify to myself what I am asking for. Thus, when I enter a challenging and uncertain situation I say, "I'm putting my trust in my faith, Dear Lord, and I am stepping out on Your Word."

I believe that each of us comes from the Creator trailing wisps of glory.

I knew that if God loved me, then I could do wonderful things, I could try great things, learn anything, achieve anything.

In all the institutions I try to be present and accountable for all I do and leave undone. I know that eventually I shall have to be present and accountable in the presence of God. I do not wish to be found wanting.

In order to survive, the ample soul needs refreshments and reminders daily of its right to be and to be wherever it finds itself.

It is Christmas time, a halting of hate time. On this platform of peace, we can create a language to translate ourselves to ourselves and to each other. At this Holy Instant, we celebrate the Birth of Christ into the great religions of the world. We jubilate the precious advent of trust. We shout with glorious tongues the coming of hope. All the earth's tribes loosen their voices to celebrate the promise of Peace.

It was hard enough to discover that I was a child of God, but to understand that the bigot and the murderer were also children of God was an even more difficult journey.

Not only was cleanliness next to godliness, dirtiness was the inventor of misery.

One person standing on the Word of God is the majority.

In the silence we listen to ourselves. Then we ask questions of ourselves. We describe ourselves to ourselves, and in the quietude we may even hear the voice of God.

Spirit is one and is everywhere present. It never leaves me. In my ignorance I may withdraw from it, but I can realize its presence the instant I return to my senses.

Stand up straight and realize who you are, that you tower over your circumstances. You are a child of God. Stand up straight.

There is a place in you that you must keep inviolate, a place that you must keep clean. A place where you say to any intruder, "Back up, don't you know I'm a child of God."

When I pray something wonderful happens, not only for the person that I am praying for, but also for me.

Whenever I begin to question whether God exists, I look up to the sky and surely there, right there, between the sun and moon, stands my grandmother, singing a long meter hymn, a song somewhere between a moan and a lullaby and I know faith is the evidence of things unseen.

GRACE

As we approach Thanksgiving—and as we experience it, and even after—I carefully maintain an attitude of gratitude. And I have changed that old saying around from "give 'til it hurts" and now I tell myself "give 'til it helps."

Continue to plant a kiss of concern on the cheek **of the sick and the aged and infirm and count that** action as natural and to be expected.

Forgiveness is the greatest gift you can give yourself.

God has been very good to me. I attempt to go everywhere spreading an attitude of gratitude.

I am much happier at receiving small gifts and more delighted to be a donor of large gifts. And all of that because I am settled in my home.

I learned that I could be a giver by simply bringing a smile to another person.

I think we must surrender the despair of unexpected cruelties and extend the wonder of unexpected kindnesses to ourselves and to each other . . . We deserve each other and each other's generosity.

It is a great blessing to have lived in the time of Martin Luther King Jr., when forgiveness and generosity of spirit encouraged our citizenry to work for a better world for everybody.

Let the brain go to work, let it meet the heart, and you will be able to forgive.

Living life as art requires a readiness to forgive.

The quality of strength lined with tenderness is an unbeatable combination.

Let gratitude be the pillow upon which you kneel to say your nightly prayer. And let faith be the bridge you build to overcome evil and welcome good.

The trouble for the receiver is not just how to accept a gift (even the gift of fame) but with what grace the recipient shares it.

To be charitable with gestures and words can bring enormous joy and repair injured feelings.

We live in direct relation to the heroes and sheroes we have. The men and women who without knowing our names or recognizing our faces, risked and sometimes gave their lives to support our country and our way of living. We must acknowledge them and say thank you.

COURAGE

Develop enough courage so that you can stand up for yourself and then stand up for somebody else.

Have enough courage to love.

> *Here then is my*
> *Christian lack:*
> *If I'm struck then*
> *I'll strike back.*

History, despite its wrenching pain, cannot be unlived, but if faced with courage, need not be lived again.

I mean to make myself more to deal with than the brute can handle.

Ignorance is not genetic. A lack of courage allows us to remain blinded to our own history and deaf to the cries of our past.

If one has courage,
nothing can dim the light
which shines from
within.

It is said that courage is the most important of all the virtues, because without courage you can't practice any other virtue with consistency.

Since a price will be exacted from us for everything we do or leave undone, we should pluck up the courage to win, to win back our finer and kinder and healthier selves.

There is no failure as long as you learn from your experience, continue to work, and continue to press on for success.

When my mother, Vivian Baxter, was confronted by challenges from fools or people she didn't like, she said, "You better say Joe, 'cause you sho' don't know." And that was a warning that needed to be heeded.

EMOTIONS

A person's speech is a mirror to her or his soul.

A textured guilt was my familiar, my bedmate to whom I had turned my back. My daily companion whose hand I would not hold.

Bitterness is like cancer. It eats upon the host.

I've learned that whenever I decide something with an open heart, I usually make the right decision. I've learned that even when I have pains, I don't have to be one. I've learned that every day you should reach out and touch someone. People love a warm hug or just a friendly pat on the back. I've learned that I still have a lot to learn.

Inordinate tears are the crystal rags and vicious tatters of a worn-out soul. Back in Stamps my grandmother used to tell me, "Sister, don't spend too much time on tears. The more you cry, the less you pee and peeing is more important." Life has since taught me a less humorous caveat: Excessive whining and tears are taken as signs of weakness by those around you and let the bully and the brute know there is a victim in the neighborhood.

Laughter and smiles are essential factors in a joyous life. The dicty folks who walk around with the backs of their hands glued to their foreheads as an indication of their sober decorum and seriousness are missing the point. A smile is a welcoming expression that allows people to approach you more easily, and laughter chases the darkness away and allows sunlight to enter your heart. Liberate yourself; smile and laugh regularly and often.

Remember your own shortcomings, and when you encounter another with flaws, don't be eager to righteously seal yourself away from the offender forever. Take a few breaths and imagine yourself having just committed the action which has set you at odds.

Some decide that happiness and glee are the same thing, they are not. When we choose happiness we accept the responsibility to lighten the load of someone else and to be a light on the path of another who may be walking in darkness.

The human heart is so delicate and sensitive that it always needs some tangible encouragement to prevent it from faltering in its labor. The human heart is so robust, so tough, that once encouraged it beats its rhythm with a loud unswerving insistency.

Those who would use ridicule as a form of humor, sow nothing but shame and bitterness and when the snide laughter ends, they will reap only anger and hostility.

Tragedy, no matter how sad, becomes boring to those not caught in its addictive caress.

You may not control all the events that happen to you, but you can decide not to be reduced by them.

You shouldn't go through life with a catcher's mitt on both hands; you need to be able to throw something back.

What you're supposed to do when you don't like a thing is change it. If you can't change it, change the way you think about it. Don't complain.

SELF-ESTEEM

Content is of great importance, but we must not underrate the value of style.

Dignity doesn't just mean always being stiff and composed. It means a belief in oneself, that one is worthy of the best. Dignity means that what I have to say is important, and I will say it when it's important for me to say it. Dignity really means that I deserve the best treatment I can receive. And that I have the responsibility to give the best treatment I can to other people.

I am never proud to participate in violence, yet I know that each of us must care enough for ourselves to be ready and able to come to our own defense.

I do my best because I'm counting on you counting on me.

I have a certain way of being in this world, and I shall not, I shall not be moved from doing what I think is right by jealousy, ignorance, or hate.

If I am comfortable inside my skin, I have the ability to make other people comfortable inside their skins.

If we have someone who loves us—I don't mean who indulges us, but who loves us enough to be on our side—then it's easier to grow resilience, to grow belief in self, to grow self-esteem. And it's self-esteem that allows a person to stand up.

It is important that we learn humility, which says there was someone else before me who paid for me. My responsibility is to prepare myself so that I can pay for someone else who is yet to come.

Once when Oprah Winfrey was upset by a story in a tabloid I encouraged her to understand, "You're not in it. People will try to peck you to death like a duck but you're not in it." That is my advice to all of you when others dare to disgrace your name.

If you are always trying to be normal, you will never know how amazing you can be.

The idea of overcoming is always fascinating to me. It's fascinating because few of us realize how much energy we have expended just to be here today. I don't think we give ourselves enough credit for the overcoming.

Try rather to be so much yourself that the clothes you choose increase your naturalness and grace.

We must stay vigilant and be very careful of how we allow ourselves to be addressed.

What I have always wanted is to be of use. I will not be abused. I will not be misused, not willingly. But I will be of use. Anybody who is not of use is useless.

You have been paid for. Each of you, Black, White, Brown, Yellow, Red—whatever pigment you use to describe yourselves—has been paid for. But for the sacrifices made by some of your ancestors, you would not be here; they have paid for you. So, when you enter a challenging situation, bring them on the stage with you; let their distant voices add timbre and strength to your words. For it is your job to pay for those who are yet to come.

My wish for you is that you continue. Continue to be who and how you are, to astonish a mean world with your acts of kindness. Continue to allow humor to lighten the burden of your tender heart.

LIVING

My hand is at the small of your back; I may let you stumble, but I will never let you fall.

All knowledge is spendable currency depending upon the market.

Bigotry, envy, greed, and ignorance do not have to be taught; these things come naturally, and if unfettered are as destructive as addictive drugs. These forces have the ability to reduce a person to nothing more than an id, and like addictive drugs their allure defies the weak to withstand their attraction.

Coming events will affect me, however my prayer and determination are that they will not reduce me.

Each of us has the right and the responsibility to assess the roads which lie ahead, and those over which we have traveled, and if the future road looms ominous or unpromising, and the roads back uninviting, then we need to gather our resolve and, carrying only the necessary baggage, step off that road into another direction.

If the new choice is also unpalatable, without embarrass-ment, we must be ready to change that as well.

Every person needs to take one day away. A day in which one consciously separates the past from the future . . . Each person deserves a day away in which no problems are confronted, no solutions searched for. Each of us needs to withdraw from the cares which will not withdraw from us . . . A day away acts as a spring tonic. It can dispel rancor, transform indecision, and renew the spirit.

Honey, tired don't mean lazy, and every good-bye ain't gone.

I agreed a long time ago, I would not live at any cost. If I am moved or forced away from what I think is the right thing, I will not do it. Yes, one must be agile and willing, but if one is being asked to contradict, one must remember there may be a difference in manner, but there must not be a difference in meaning.

I had been asked what I would like as my last meal if I was going to die. I had replied, "I don't want to think that far ahead, but if I were going to Mars tomorrow I would like to have hot chicken, a chilled bottle of white wine, and a loaf of good bread."

I love a Hebrew National hot dog with an ice-cold Corona—no lime. If the phone rings, I won't answer until I'm done.

I'll protest like the dickens, but I don't complain. After hearing someone complain, my grandmother would say, "There are people all over the world, Black and White, rich and poor, who went to sleep when that person went to sleep, and they have never awakened. They would give anything for five minutes of what that person was complaining about."

It is always about the work. In the latter years of your life, your happiness and your self-esteem will be determined by the mountains you surmounted, the valleys you climbed out of, and the life and/or career that you forged for yourself.

Joy is an important element of happiness. It is sometimes the difference between striving and thriving. One must nurture the joy in one's life so that it reaches full bloom.

Mostly, what I have learned so far about aging, despite the creakiness of one's bones and the cragginess of one's once-silken skin, is this: do it. By all means, do it.

One must contrive to keep innocence in one's life, how else is one to continue to enjoy the simple things such as sunrises, sunsets, or the acknowledging smile of a passing stranger?

Since life is our most precious gift
And since it is given to us to live but once,
Let us so live that we will not regret
Years of uselessness and inertia.

The problem for the thief is not how to steal the trumpet, but where to blow it.

There were times when it was said that I had more determination than talent. This may be said of many. It may also be said that life loves the person who dares to live it.

We delight in the beauty of the butterfly, but rarely admit the changes it has gone through to achieve that beauty.

We owe the truth, not just the facts. The facts can sometimes obscure the truth. I've seen many things. I've learned many things. I've certainly been exposed to many things and I've learned something: I owe it to you to tell you.

When I sense myself filling with rage at the absence of a beloved, I try as soon as possible to remember that my concerns and questions, my efforts and answers should be focused on what I did or can learn from my departed love. What legacy was left which can help me in the art of living a good life?

WOMANHOOD

A rose by any other name may smell as sweet, but a woman called by a devaluing name will only be weakened by the misnomer.

A woman is careful with judgment, is courteous, has courage, and is much given to kindness, support, and respect for other women.

And my breasts—it's better not to mention them at all except to say that they seemed to be in a race to see which could be first to reach my knees.

Being a woman is hard work. Not without joy and even ecstasy, but still relentless, unending work. Becoming an old female may require only being born with certain genitalia, inheriting long-living genes, and the fortune not to be run over by an out-of-control truck, but to become and remain a woman command the existence and employment of genius.

Each time a woman stands up for herself, without knowing it possibly, without claiming it, she stands up for all women.

I had long known that there were worlds of difference between males and men, as there were between females and women. Genitalia indicated sex, but work, discipline, courage, and love were needed for the creation of men and women.

I wanted to be a wife and to create a beautiful home to make my man happy, but there was more to life than being a diligent maid with a permanent pussy.

I'd rather be an old man's darling than a young man's slave.

It is imperative that a woman keep her sense of humor intact and at the ready. She must see, even if only in secret, that she is the funniest, looniest woman in her world, which she should also see as being the most absurd world of all times.

My mother says a woman who will tell her own age will tell anything.

She spends half her time making herself attractive to men, and the other half trying to divine which of the attracted are serious enough to marry her, and which wish to ram her against the nearest wall and jab into her recklessly.

The Black mother perceives destruction at every door, ruination at each window, and even she herself is not beyond her own suspicion. She questions whether she loves her children enough—or more terribly, does she love them too much? Do her looks cause embarrassment—or even more terrifying, is she so attractive her sons begin to desire her and her daughters begin to hate her? If she is unmarried, the challenges are increased. Her singleness indicates she has rejected or has been rejected by her mate. Yet she is raising children who will become mates. Beyond her door, all authority is in the hands of people who do not look or think or act like her and her children.

Let me remind all women that we live longer and better lives when we have sisters we love, not necessarily born in our bloodline or of our race.

The heartbreaking tenderness of Black women and their majestic strength speak of the heroic survival of a people who were stolen into subjugation, denied chastity, and refused innocence.

The wise woman thinks twice and speaks once or, better yet, does not speak at all.

The woman who survives intact and happy must be at once tender and tough. She must have convinced herself, or be in the unending process of convincing herself, that she, her values, and her choices are important. In a time and world where males hold sway and control, the pressure upon women to yield their rights-of-way is tremendous. And it is under those very circumstances that the woman's toughness must be in evidence.

We may act sophisticated and worldly but I believe we feel safest when we go inside ourselves and find home, a place where we belong and maybe the only place we really do.

When old folks laugh,
they free the world.

WORKS CITED

All God's Children Need Traveling Shoes

19 The Black child   27 Black Americans
29 Malcolm   30 Prejudice is   31 Since we were
33 Through the centuries   33 Unbidden would
come   34 Whites had been wrong   38 African and
Southern Black   42 The Stars and Stripes   47 All
people use   59 The thorn from   65 Art was the
76 In order to survive   102 Tragedy, no matter
130 I had long known   131 My mother says

And Still I Rise

29 I was born   57 Love, by nature

Even the Stars Look Lonesome Tonight

19 Parents who tell   19 This is no longer
28 Black women whose   34 We must ask
50 Together, we may   55 From the moment
57 Leers and lascivious   66 If a little learning
66 In that little town   69 We must be suspicious

135

had   32 The drums began   39 Appearances to the
130 I wanted to   131 The Black mother

Wouldn't Take Nothing for My Journey Now

18 If our children   18 It is time   20 Our young
must   48 Perhaps travel   55 A conversation   56 I
try to plant   57 Jealousy in romance   78 Spirit is
one   84 Living life as   93 Since a price
100 Remember your own   103 What you're
supposed   109 Content is   109 I am never proud
110 If I am comfortable   112 Try rather to
112 We must stay   119 Each of us   120 Every
person needs   124 When I sense   129 A rose by
129 Being a woman   130 It is imperative
133 The woman who

WE ARE ESPECIALLY GRATEFUL TO GUY Johnson and the Estate of Maya Angelou, who contributed invaluable material and guidance to this project. During a time filled with immeasurable grief, Mr. Johnson stepped through his own mourning to help curate a project that would help the world pay tribute to his mother, and to make these pages sing with her signature voice.

PHOTOGRAPH PERMISSIONS

ABOUT THE AUTHOR

MAYA ANGELOU WAS RAISED IN STAMPS, Arkansas. In addition to her bestselling auto-biographies, including *I Know Why the Caged Bird Sings* and *The Heart of a Woman*, she wrote numerous volumes of poetry, among them *Phenomenal Woman*, *And Still I Rise*, *On the Pulse of Morning*, and *Mother*. Maya Angelou died in 2014.

Center Point Large Print
600 Brooks Road / PO Box 1
Thorndike, ME 04986-0001 USA

(207) 568-3717

US & Canada:
1 800 929-9108
www.centerpointlargeprint.com